Stockpo
IN THE DAYS OF
STEAM

To Ray, Best Wishes from Paul

The architectural splendour of Stockport Tiviot Dale Station was matched in the immediate vicinity by Hanover Congregational Chapel and School. These are the buildings directly behind the loco, beyond which, on the other side of Lancashire Hill, stands the equally impressive Pendlebury Hall which can be glimpsed through the signal arms. Stanier Class 4MT 2-6-4T No **42491** has arrived at its destination, having worked the 10.15am local passenger train from Warrington Central over the CLC. With the closure of Brunswick (Liverpool) shed on 12th September 1961, these duties became the joint responsibility of Speke Junction and Heaton Mersey depots for the final three years. This particular locomotive was allocated to Speke Junction (8C) from April 1963 until its withdrawal five months later.

11th JULY 1963 ● G.HARROP

PAUL SHACKCLOTH

Stockport
IN THE DAYS OF
STEAM

First published 2002

ISBN 0 9543128 0 5

Published by Steam Image, PO Box 90, Cheadle Hulme, Cheshire SK8 6WZ and printed by Deanprint Ltd, Stockport, Cheshire SK3 0PR.

FOREWORD

The County Borough of Stockport possesses a proud and fascinating history and the railway network within its boundary has certainly played a part. Set on the sprawling fringe of south Manchester, it was at one time in danger of being swallowed up within that city's greater conurbation. To its eternal credit, the town remained fiercely independent, not only retaining but enhancing its own identity.

Stockport, however, represented a thorn in the side for the railway builders of the early constituent companies. They were faced with different challenges. The major North - South route was compelled to straddle the Mersey Valley. This of course was overcome by construction of a 27 - arch brick viaduct, whilst the route from East to West offered contrasting problems and a combination of embankment, cutting and tunnel sufficed. The railways of Stockport have been well documented over the years but the diversity of traffic on both the ex LNWR and CLC lines made for rich pickings for the photographer. The ex Midland main line passes within the boundary in the Cheadle Heath area as does the ex GC Fallowfield line on which stood Reddish Electric Depot, constructed as late as 1954. Both routes offer further variety. Much, of course, has long since disappeared and it is now hard to imagine that a line ever existed in the Heaton Mersey and Tiviot Dale area where the M60 motorway cuts a swathe through the town on land once occupied by the CLC.

I make no excuse for the pictorial content being the hero. This photographic essay seeks to complement other work and is not meant in any way to be definitive. I have attempted to assemble a balanced selection of photographs, the majority of which remain unpublished. Many of the captions have a topographical flavour which I trust will be of interest to both the historian and enthusiast alike. The town's alternative form of public transport, the major bus operators Stockport Corporation and North Western Road Car Co Ltd also receive and deserve a presence.

From the outset I made a conscious decision to restrict the scope of material mostly to views within the town's boundary. They offer a nostalgic look back, mainly during the latter years of steam, but the few that are included outside the Borough feature only Stockport Edgeley or Heaton Mersey locomotives. If the title of the book appears to be misleading in this respect, I apologise.

ACKNOWLEDGEMENTS

A work such as this would have been impossible without the help of many people and I am deeply indebted to the many photographers who have allowed me to make use of their material. Particular thanks must go to David Harrop for making available much of the excellent work of his late father, Gerald Harrop. In a similar vein, Jean Bentley has kindly allowed me to reproduce images from the collection of her late husband Eric Bentley, as has Bernard Crick regarding the late Tom Morgan's photographs. Brian Green, as well as providing a selection of his own excellent photographs, has also supplied those of the late Jim Davenport. Another eminent local steam cameraman was the late Tom Lewis and many of his shots appear courtesy of Norman Preedy and Ray Hinton.

Others who have freely contributed in various ways include Arthur Haynes, David Young, Trevor Moseley, Michael Keeley, Liz Pearce (*Stockport Express*), Gordon Coltas, Joe Leighton and John Hales. To both write and produce a book is a time consuming business and as a consequence, I must acknowledge the odd inconvenience placed upon the Shackcloth family, especially on my wife Norma, whose patience knows no bounds (so far!)

AUGUST 2002 ● PAUL SHACKCLOTH

DEDICATION

I wish to dedicate this book to my father, Joe Shackcloth who was responsible for fostering his son's interest in railways from an early age. During the 1950's whilst on family holidays at Great Yarmouth, dad would often take young Paul to Caister Station on the old M&GN line to stand near the level crossing ready to watch the 9.00am to Leicester go by. B12 No 61540 remains a fond, yet distant memory.

Both driver and fireman look cautiously down Platform 2 at Reddish South Station as the 6.50pm local train from Stalybridge to Stockport draws to its penultimate stop. The loco is one of Stockport Edgeley's stud of 2-6-4 Fowler Tanks, No **42391**. Goods traffic is still much in evidence although there is little sign of the north end of Platforms 3 and 4 which once occupied land to the right of the engine.

22nd JUNE 1962 ● **G. COLTAS**

Rising majestically out of the Reddish skyline stands Broadstone Mill. Built by the Broadstone Spinning Company between the years 1903-7, it stood alongside *The Manchester, Ashton and Oldham Canal* which had opened some 110 years earlier. This waterway branch from Clayton became the property of *The Manchester, Sheffield and Lincolnshire Railway* in 1848 and carried its last revenue earning barge in 1934. Broadstone Mill closed some years later in 1959. The train is the 8.00am ex Colne which has arrived in the Stockport area by way of Burnley, Blackburn, Bolton, Manchester Victoria and Droylsden Junction and has through carriages for London. They went forward from Stockport Edgeley as part of the 10.15am Manchester London Road - London Euston service. On summer Saturdays in earlier years it ran through to London as a separate train, combining with through carriages from Halifax. A restaurant car was attached between sections by the Edgeley pilot. A Longsight Royal Scot or Patriot was rostered to run light engine to Edgeley before taking the train forward. The loco pictured is Accrington Class Five 4-6-0 No **44692** with the rearmost carriages of the train passing over the canal bridge. **6th OCTOBER 1959** ● **R. KEELEY**

A type of locomotive long associated with Stockport Edgeley Depot was the ex LNWR "Super D' Class 0-8-0. Here No **49453,** running tender first, has a BR standard brake van for company and is heading in the Guide Bridge direction. This combination constituted a train whose guard, whilst keeping a watchful eye on progress, has correctly positioned the tail lamp before departure. A similar 'train' is approaching on the Down Fast line as an unidentified Hughes 'Crab' 2-6-0 brings an earlier LMS type brake van towards Stockport.

6th OCTOBER 1959 ● **R. KEELEY**

ASH BRIDGE

An unidentified Class Five heads north towards Reddish on the main line with a van train and is seen passing under the original bridge. Ash Bridge Signal Box is just in view to the right of the engine whilst the Empress Club may be glimpsed in the background. Further down Manchester Road and beyond the allotments stands the Ash Hotel on the far left. Opening in 1820, this public house was originally the Ash Inn and brewed its own beer. The Ash Brewery closed in 1900.

18th OCTOBER 1967 ● P. SHACKCLOTH

The signalboxes between Heaton Norris Junction and Denton Junction were 'switched out' on Sundays when traffic density was lighter. As a consequence, the signalmen at the intermediate boxes cleared all their main running line signals to the 'off' position at the end of their shifts on Saturdays. In this Sunday view, the Ash Bridge Down Fast and Slow gantry signals together with the Up Fast and Slow Starters in the background are all 'off'. The Goods or Slow lines are on the right but prior to 1959 they handled some of the local passenger services which used Platforms 3 and 4 at Reddish South Station a mile or so ahead. Broadstone Mill, whose twin chimneys were demolished in 1964, looms on the horizon.

18th OCTOBER 1967 ● P. SHACKCLOTH

One late afternoon in August 1966, Stockport Corporation Crossley No **324** pulls away from its stop on Ash Bridge itself. Although aptly bound for Stockport, Crossley Road, the bus carries no route number but is probably working a 47 from Cheadle Heath (or possibly Mersey Square) as a rush hour extra. Passengers on the top deck would have been treated to a splendid view of Jubilee Sidings at this point to the right of the photograph.

17th AUGUST 1966 ● P. SHACKCLOTH

Many of the BR Standard 9F 2-10-0's started work on the ex Midland lines based at depots such as Wellingborough, Kettering, Toton and Leicester. In 1955 and 1956 a trio of locos came north from Wellingborough to Bidston specifically for work on the Shotton iron ore traffic. Nos 92045/6 and 7, then barely a year old, were destined to spend the rest of their days on the Wirral. When the tiny Bidston depot closed on 11th February 1963 all three moved up the road to Birkenhead, a much larger depot which became well associated with the class in later years. No **92047** bursts out from under Ash Bridge with Yorkshire bound mineral empties. The Empress Club, beyond the bridge, started life in May 1939 as a cinema and was the last example to be built in the town. Cabaret and Bingo ruled the roost from 1959 until a fire in May 1967 brought about the club's premature closure. It re-opened in December 1968 as the Poco-a-Poco Club and Casino by which time steam on BR was but a memory.

1966 ● T. RENSHAW

Major industrial premises which played their part in the town's heritage lie on the horizon, just within the Borough boundary. In this view looking north towards Levenshulme, the Crossley Motor Company, situated in Errwood Park lies to the left. They were responsible for producing large numbers of buses, many of which were supplied for the two Corporations' municipal bus fleets after the war. The factory, which had rail access via a private siding, closed in 1957. The premises opposite were those of the McVitie & Price Biscuit Works. Opening in 1917, a merger with Macfarlane Lang led to the formation of United Biscuits in 1948. The aroma emanating from the bakery was no doubt appreciated by photographer Tom Lewis as he recorded the passage of Fowler Class 4MT 2-6-4T No **2306** approaching Heaton Chapel and Heaton Moor Station on the Up fast line with a local train to Crewe.

13th JUNE 1949 ● T. LEWIS

An interesting working during the 1950's was the 6.05pm Manchester Mayfield to Stockport Edgeley local train. This was regularly in the hands of one of Longsight's ten 'Jinties' as a means of getting the loco to its required destination. On arrival it then ran light to Jubilee Sidings, Heaton Norris, to commence pilot duties. Although Edgeley shed, barely a mile away, had three examples on its books, they confined their activities to Edgeley Junction and Adswood Sidings. Introduced in 1924, 0-6-0T No **47343** has left Heaton Chapel and Heaton Moor Station and is nearing Heaton Norris Junction. By the end of 1960 members of this diminutive class had been either withdrawn or transferred away from both depots.

4th JUNE 1954 ● B.K.B. GREEN

An engine whose name carried a local significance was Longsight's Rebuilt Patriot 4-6-0 No **45536** *Private W. Wood V.C.* Wilf Wood worked as a cleaner at Edgeley shed before the Great War intervened. He received the Victoria Cross for bravery whilst in action after which he resumed his railway career, gravitating to Running Foreman at Longsight Shed. The 'Pat', named in his honour, is in charge of a heavy Manchester London Road to London Euston express made up of a smart set of carmine & cream carriages. A pair of BR Mark 1 examples are sandwiched between the standard LMS types. Heaton Moor Road bridge is in the distance immediately beyond which lies the station. Just discernable through the bridge between the Down and Up Fast lines is a small 12 lever signal box split into two banks of six facing the oncoming traffic in either direction - an unusual arrangement.

4th JUNE 1954 ● B.K.B. GREEN

The arrival of a Coronation Pacifi[c] was usually the highlight of a trainspotte[r's] day spent perched on Bowerfold La[ne] bridge. Popularly known as 'Duchesse[s]' or 'Semis' they were regular visitors, ve[ry] often on running in turns from Crew[e] Works. A gentle stroll with six c[oaches] through the Cheshire countryside w[as] ideal preparation for the more serio[us] work to come - the assaults on Sha[p] and Beattock. No **46228 Duchess** [of] **Rutland,** a Carlisle Upperby loco, [is] bound for London Road Station.

21st MAY 1956 ● T. LEW[IS]

HEATON NORRIS JUNCTION

In 1955, BR introduced colour light signalling in the Heaton Norris area prior to the electrification scheme between Manchester and Crewe which was to follow some five years later. This splendid photograph, looking north towards Manchester, was taken six months earlier from Bowerfold Lane Bridge whose five arches spanned the complexity of running lines. The only hint of change is the shell of the new architect designed box lurking menacingly behind Heaton Norris Junction signal box. Having deposited its train in nearby Jubilee Sidings, a 'Super D' 0-8-0 ambles along and joins the Up slow line on its way to Edgeley shed. Another member of the class can be seen resting between duties in the background. Anyone unfamiliar with the area could be mistaken for thinking an ex-LNWR shed was lurking out of sight to the right. The water tower was, in fact, a hydraulic accumulator built to serve the imposing Heaton Norris goods warehouse which was situated on the east side of the Up main line immediately south of Bowerfold Lane bridge. The tracks veering off to the right offered several important links. From here, the quadruple five mile stretch of line passed through Reddish South and Denton Stations before reaching Denton Junction where it split three ways. That via Droylsden Junction offered a connection with Manchester's Victoria Station and all towns north of the city. The route via Hooley Hill through Stalybridge gave access to Yorkshire and beyond. The direct line fed the Guide Bridge area whose station was seemingly surrounded by a maze of lines. The LNWR used to boast that it had the best permanent way in the world, a reputation upheld in latter years by both the LMS and BR. From this photograph it would be difficult to argue.

4th JUNE 1954 ● **B.K.B. GREEN**

A Rose Grove Crab 2-6-0 No 42706 brings a Wakefield - Belle Vue excursion into Heaton Norris Station The train, comprising 10 corridor coaches, will reverse here with another engine taking over for the last five miles of the journey. It will cross over on to the Down slow line, passing through Heaton Chapel and Levenshulme stations before arriving at the Longsight for Belle Vue excursion platform. 42706, in the meantime, will proceed light engine over the viaduct and on to Edgeley shed for turning and servicing prior to its return journey to Yorkshire later in the day.   **c.1956** ● **J. DAVENPORT**

HEATON NORRIS JUNCTION

A busy spell sees Austerity 2-8-0 No **90322** from Farnley Junction bringing a mixed selection of wagons around the 'bucket' from Yorkshire on to the Up slow line. Meanwhile Stanier Class 4 2-6-4T No **42551** working bunker first, takes the Colne train formed from the five rear carriages of a Euston - London Road express which were detached at Edgeley Station. Trains on the main line to Manchester were invariably given priority by Heaton Norris Junction signalmen.

c.1956 ● **J. DAVENPORT**

One of Longsight's immaculate Royal Scots, 7P 4-6-0 No **46169** *The Boy Scout* rattles over the diamond crossing by Heaton Norris Junction Box with an Up express for London Euston. The different carriage liveries are of interest. The corridor stock of carmine and cream contrasts starkly with the all crimson lake used for non-gangwayed examples whose compartments comfortably accomodated twelve adult passengers sitting six abreast. This is a five coach set forming a local service from Stalybridge to Stockport Edgeley slowing down for its penultimate stop at Heaton Norris's number one platform. Belmont Bridge, carrying Wellington Road North (the A6) is just in view above the loco.

c.1956 ● **B.K.B. GREEN**

HEATON NORRIS JUNCTION

A classic view taken from Bowerfold Lane bridge. Both trains are signalled for the Guide Bridge direction. The local passenger has Edgeley's Stanier Class 3 2-6-2T No **40081** in charge which will take the slow line calling first at Reddish South station. On its right, Stanier 8F 2-8-0 No **48289** (5B - Crewe South) takes to the fast line with vans which may be merely transferring over the town from Adswood to Jubilee Sidings. If so, they will set back by Ash Bridge signal box or otherwise the train will proceed in a north easterly direction.

C.1954 ● J. DAVENPORT

The Down 'Comet'. Yet another rebuilt Patriot 4-6-0' belonging to Longsight, No **45530 Sir Frank Ree,** picks up speed after its penultimate stop at Stockport Edgeley and is seen passing through the deserted platforms of Heaton Norris Station. This photograph oozes railway atmosphere with the busy Wellington Road Goods Warehouse prominent and is highlighted by the magnificent array of ex-LNWR bracket signals, all sited to be in clear view for engine crews crossing the viaduct with northbound traffic. Heaton Norris No 1 Signal box is situated at the north end of island platforms 2 and 3 and is seen alongside the fourth coach. Meanwhile, the lengthy mixed goods train seen threading its way southbound may well be a transfer freight from Jubilee Sidings to Adswood Sidings, situated some 2 miles beyond Edgeley Station on the Down side of the main line to Cheadle Hulme.

c.1954 ● J. DAVENPORT

A similar view shortly after the 1955 re-signalling scheme. The array of semaphores have been replaced by standard cantilever colour light signals. Of particular interest are the signal heads on the slow line. Because of the multiple routes the train could take, it was considered necessary to provide an additional signal head alongside the main one. Stanier 8F No **48554** (8D - Widnes) makes for Manchester with a mineral train whose wagons are predominantly the older, wooden variety. Two clerestory coaches standing on the Signal and Telegraph depot sidings act as mess vans for the S&T Gang Staff whilst working within the district. Their premises are also just in view.

c.1956 ● J. DAVENPORT

A few Caprotti Class Fives added even more variety to the Longsight allocation. Here, No **44749** is striding out towards London Road with a train from the West of England.

c.1954 ● J. DAVENPORT

HEATON NORRIS STATION

Uttoxeter provided Fowler Class 4 2-6-4 tanks for certain Manchester trains. No **42375** passes through Platform 3 on its homeward journey.

c.1954 ● J. DAVENPORT

The station is seen here during its last week of service, closing on 2nd March 1959. A Birmingham RC+W three car set is passing through Platform 1 and these units were often used on the Uttoxeter route before the service was withdrawn. With the station clock showing 4.05pm and no train being booked to pass at, or near to that time, it is safe to assume it was no longer in working order. One wonders whether it survived or, indeed, was part of the original building dating from 1840. Note the rather ornate gas lamps on an otherwise spartan island platform which had closed some time beforehand, access from the subway which originally served all four platforms having been sealed off. Passenger services via the Churnet Valley ceased when the North Rode to Leek section closed on 7th November 1960. Freight traffic lingered on until 15th June 1964 at which time the line closed completely.

25th FEBRUARY 1959 ● D. R. MORGAN

Road Motor Drivers Billy Gilligan (left) **and George Royle** (centre), in the company of an unidentified checker, look none too happy as they contemplate the situation on a bitterly cold morning. When overnight frosts were forecast, drivers were instructed to drain off the radiators before leaving for home. There was every likelihood that this Karrier Bantam wouldn't start. Anti-freeze was eventually introduced by BR in 1969. **c.1968 ● D. JESSOP**

Checker Andy Goulden casts an inquisitive eye in the direction of the photographer on the same morning whilst colleagues report for duty in the unheated warehouse. The 3 ton Scammell Scarab in the foreground had received minor front end damage in the yard whilst a further three Karrier Bantams stand within and around the entrance. **c.1968 ● D. JESSOP**

WELLINGTON ROAD NORTH GOODS DEPOT

Checker Raymond Boswell takes advantage of one of the three fires positioned in the yard near the capstans. They kept the ropes and chains warm as they were susceptible to snapping at low temperatures.

c.1968 ● D. JESSOP

An everyday sight on the streets of Stockport during the 1960's were the much loved 3 ton Scammell Scarabs. This preserved 1959 example is in British Railways livery.

c.1980 ● K. TEASDALE

Wellington Road North Goods Depot, that most imposing of buildings, was built by the LNWR primarily for the cotton trade and opened its doors in 1882. A depot of such magnitude reflected the ever growing importance of Stockport as a railway centre to handle increasing amounts of goods gravitating to the town.

Early forms of transport were horse and cart. Up to 40 horses were available and were tended to by an ostler, a minuted position that commanded a higher rate of pay than a carter. The stables on the premises were constantly manned. On the outbreak of war in 1939 the depot fell victim to an air raid attack on December 22nd 1940. This was the only damage suffered on railway property in the Borough but a direct hit on the goods yard resulted in extensive damage to the stables. As a consequence, new facilities were provided at the rear of the neighbouring CLC Georges Road Sidings.

The depot's situation, however, presented problems. Standing adjacent to Stockport's original station, Heaton Norris, the building ran alongside Wellington Road North which was the main north - south thoroughfare. This represented a 500 yard climb up the north side of the Mersey valley. As a consequence, a pair of 'chain' horses were daily deployed to assist heavy loads on the final stage of their journey. Many a local 'tatter' also benefitted from unofficial assistance up the hill, much to the chagrin of authority. These 'Pilot' horses were tethered by the water troughs on Gas Street, opposite *The Touchstone* public house by Mersey Square. Other water troughs could be found at the junction of Higher Hillgate and London Road (opposite the *Blossoms Hotel*) and by *The Rising Sun Inn*, Hazel Grove which remained in situ for many years after the horses' demise.

The warehouse from a distance. Looking easterly from Green Lane on Hope Hill, the gardens and reservoir (just out of view), lie within the Bowerfold open space. On the other side of Wellington Road North, the spire of St. Thomas's towers high above, Acting almost as a centrepiece, this also became a listed specimen. If the photographer were to turn south, he would be overlooking Club House Sidings on the CLC beyond which lay Travis Brow in the Brinksway District of Stockport in the Mersey valley.

c.1963 ● STOCKPORT EXPRESS

The introduction of motor transport brought about inevitable change and by 1942 the depot's fleet were 20 road motors supported by a stud of 25 horses. A significant change was the arrival of the ubiquitous 3 wheeled Scammell Scarabs. Introduced in 1951, the models were manufactured at Watford works. The smaller 3 ton vehicle had a turning circle equivalent to that of a horse and was one man operated. A number of the earlier models were fitted with isinglass curtains and canvas doors whereas the larger 6 ton version required the services of two men. The Depot received their first batch of these vehicles in 1953 by which time the days of the horse and cart were numbered. Interestingly, the stone setts on the section of road from Mersey Square up Wellington Road North remained at a time when many were receiving their first helpings of tarmacadam. These setts greatly assisted the 'double headers' up the hill.

With the closure of Macclesfield (1964), Buxton (1971) and New Mills (1971) Goods Depots, Wellington Road experienced an Indian summer having to deal with all manner of re-directed traffic, but by the late 1970's the writing was on the wall. Closure came in July 1981 with all goods being concentrated at Manchester's Oldham Road Depot. Several employees transferred there, some opted for early retirement and redundancy packages whilst others left for pastures new.

The building is now privately owned having no rail access. Thankfully it is a Grade 2 listed structure thus preserving not only its architectural splendour but the very reason for its existence. The words LONDON AND NORTH WESTERN RAILWAY GOODS WAREHOUSE remain prominently displayed over the upper windows which serve to remind the travelling public of its historical significance.

John Hales worked at the depot throughout the 1950's. Some of the staff with whom he was associated are as follows:

CLERICAL STAFF

Goods Agent	**G.Torr** *(in overall control)*
Clerks, Shipping	C. Allen, H. English,
	C. Cook, H. Hope
Clerks, Townsman	F. Hassell, G. Shaw
Clerks, Delivery	H. Winder, C. Woods,
	R. McCarthy,
Clerk, Forwarding	E. Barnes
Clerks, Staff	J. Killoran, T. Gibons
Clerks, General	T. Rowlands, D. Woods,
	K. McCann, M. Smith,
	A. Worsley, B. Robinson,
	J. Tallant, J. Higginbotham,
	M. Bailey, J. Gartside
Cashier	F. Slack
Timekeeper/	
Weighbridge Man	E. Penney
Office Boys	K. Moss, T. Short

FULL LOAD STAFF

Checker	A. Swindells
Porter	H. King
Forwarding Gang	E. Miller, W.Smith,
	B. Kirkman, J. Winter,
	R. Boswell, D. Smith
Capstan Operatives	J. Marsland, A. Warhurst,
	C. Francis, M. Dunn

ROAD MOTOR DRIVERS

J. Brown, H. Dennerley, J. Wild, P. McGrane, N. Worthington, J. Howard, F. Nixon, J. Amos J. Williams, J. Hulme, G. Howard, T. Doyle, J. Fiddler, W. Taylor, G. Brocklehurst, T. Tymm W. Collier, C. Fantom, H. Bartles, T. Firth, T. Bradbury, W. Hopkinson, F. Dooley, S. Collingwood, F. Arrandale, J. McCormack, E. Gaskell, P. Boardman, G. Pinchbeck, G. Royle, A. Wood, J. Pownall

CARTERS

B. Pollitt, F. Hallett, J. Buck, F. Chantrel, W. Oakes, A. Sidebotham, J. Lenahan, E. Ball R. Stubbs, J. Firth, A. Gleave, J. Gladwin

OTHER STAFF

Senior Checkers	P. James, M. Burton
Lorry Loaders	B. Holt, J. Wallace,
	J. Broome, J. Hales,
	J. Shotton, F. Sherwood
Checkers	A. Goulding, J. Donlan,
	J. Warren
Porters	J. Cahill, E. Frost, A. Dean,
	J. McNamee, H. Bethell
General Duties	N. McCann

There was also a Canteen Supervisor who had 4 assistants under her control. Additionally, casual labour was often prevalent.

During the late 1940's, early 1950's period, it was considered newsworthy if a member of the local community was about to emigrate - especially to Australia. The clerical staff assemble in the goods yard to record such an occasion for the local press. Employed for a number of years as a cleaner, *Mrs Rolfe* from nearby Parsonage Street sits front row, centre stage, whilst to her immediate right is her superior, Goods Agent *Mr George Torr.* Heaton Norris No 1 Signalbox is visible behind the vans.

1951 ● STOCKPORT EXPRESS

Approaching Heaton Norris Station under clear signals on the Down Fast Line with a Manchester bound train is Stanier Pacific No **46247** *City of Liverpool.* Of note are the two fine examples of LNW bracket signals, the left one due to restricted clearance carries both Up Fast and Down Fast Line signals whilst the right hand one has the Down Slow Line signals. The straight post example on the end of Platform 1 was the Up Slow Line Starting Signal to Stockport, which carried Stockport No 2 Distant. Prior to the 1955 colour signalling scheme Heaton Norris had three signalboxes within close proximity, such was the complexity of the area. The Up Fast Starting Signal was the crucial signal that was passed in dense fog by a Buxton bound commuter train on the night of 30th November 1948, resulting in the rear end collision with a Crewe bound train on Stockport viaduct where 5 persons lost their lives and a further 26 suffered varying degrees of injury. **1951 ● T. MORGAN**

STANIER 'DUCHESSES' GRACE THE TOWN

Stanier 8P 4-6-2 Coronation Pacific No 46254, *City of Stoke-on-Trent* brings the Up *'Comet'* off the viaduct and into Platform 2 at Stockport Edgeley. The use of "Duchesses" on Friday evenings only began in late 1956/early 1957 when this train was strengthened to cater for the higher demand. This put the load beyond an unassisted Class 7P loco if the schedule was to be adhered to, so Crewe North shed sent one of its stud to work the train. In 1956 the restaurant car express departed from Manchester London Road at 5.50pm and ran via Crewe to London Euston (arr 9.20pm) calling at Stockport Edgeley, Crewe and Watford Junction only. The engine returned the following day with the 11.45am London Euston to Manchester London Road, again via Crewe. It is noteworthy that both trains took this route rather than the more direct Stoke line from which Stanier's Pacifics were prohibited at the time. **11th MAY 1962 ● G. COLTAS**

WELLINGTON ROAD SOUTH

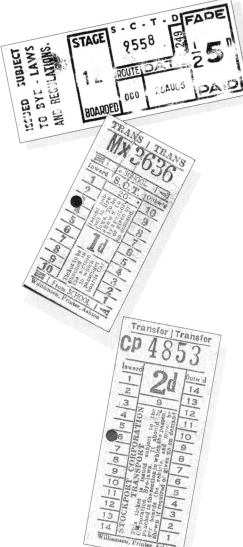

In **1958 Stockport Corporation** took delivery of four Leyland Tiger Cubs with Crossley bodies to replace buses of 1937 vintage, specifically to work Stockport's only single-deck route. Service No 75, running between Green End and Offerton was converted to double-deck operation in October 1964 and, in preparation, Crossley No 226 (JA 7626) became a tree-lopping vehicle. Tiger Cub No **401** (NDB 354) is seen approaching Mersey Square behind which lies the CLC Wellington Street Goods Depot. Notice the period litter bin on the pavement by the cyclist coasting down the hill. Over the road stands a railwayman in the company of a lady passenger awaiting the arrival of a Manchester bound bus. Further up Wellington Road North is a North Western Guy Arab working the 28 Manchester - Hayfield limited stop service.

c.1961 ● A. HAYNES COLLECTION

The bus routes plying the busy Wellington Road North in the early 1960's were as follows:

SERVICE	ROUTE	OPERATOR/S
18	Manchester - Dialstone Lane (Limited Stop)	Manchester and Stockport Corporation
20	Manchester - Poynton (Limited Stop)	Manchester, Stockport Corporation and North Western
20A	Manchester - Woodford (Limited Stop)	Manchester, Stockport Corporation and North Western
27	Manchester - Buxton (Limited Stop)	North Western
28	Manchester - Hayfield (Limited Stop)	North Western
75	Green End - Offerton	Stockport Corporation
89	Manchester - Stockport	Manchester and Stockport Corporation
92	Manchester - Hazel Grove	Manchester and Stockport Corporation
X1	Manchester - Derby (Express)	North Western and Trent
X2	Manchester - Nottingham (Express)	North Western and Trent
X5	Manchester - London (Express)	North Western and Midland Red
X67	Manchester - Chesterfield (Express)	North Western and East Midland

Additionally, many excursions offering a rich variety of buses and coaches from various companies, ran by way of the A6 particularly on summer Saturdays.

HEATON LANE DEPOT

After the war, Crossley Motors chose to concentrate bus production at their Heaton Chapel factory in Errwood Park. They supplied chassis and bodywork (often both) to various municipalities, not least to Stockport and the neighbouring Corporation of Manchester who took delivery of large numbers of buses and trolleybuses. Stockport operated two MCTD style streamlined Crossleys of pre-war design. These were Nos 203 and 205 which were ordered in 1939 but not delivered until 1941. The first post war vehicles were built in 1946/7 and carried fleet numbers 207/ 225 - 244, closely followed by 245 - 264 in 1948. The third and last batch were 309 - 332 delivered in 1951. The factory ceased production and closed in 1957. Stockport Corporation's bus fleet was 148 vehicles strong in October 1963 of which 64 were Crossleys. No **256** (CJA 780) stands in the yard between duties at Heaton Lane Depot.

The view towards Manchester from the platform end. Two trains are simultaneously held at the gantry, awaiting the signal for entry into Edgeley station. On the Up Slow line *(far right)*, a Fowler 2-6-4 Tank has charge of a local service to either Buxton or Macclesfield. Alongside on the Up Fast is a Stanier loco, no doubt working an express turn. Meanwhile the station pilot, a Stanier 2-6-2T, has the road to reverse back into the station area. The bell mouth allowed the lines to immediately fan out into the platforms, loops and carriage sidings. On the parapet, to the right is a brass plaque commemorating the construction of the 'old' viaduct between 10th March 1839 and 16th July 1841.

7th JUNE 1952 ● R. S. CARPENTER

STOCKPORT
VIADUCT

An interesting variety of North Western Road Car vehicles stand in Daw Bank Bus Park awaiting their next journeys whilst high above, Stanier 8F 2-8-0 No **48321** brings a southbound mixed freight over Stockport's most notable landmark. Dominating the town centre, this 27 arch brick built structure is 1,780ft in length with all but 5 of those arches having a span of 63ft.

MAY 1966 ● T. RENSHAW

Although the first locomotive passed over the 'old' viaduct on 16th July 1841, by 1885 some 250 passenger and 140 goods trains were daily traversing the double track. To ease this congestion, a 'new' viaduct was constructed between 1887 and 1890 to the immediate West or Down side, resulting in the running lines being quadrupled. The increased intensity of traffic often resulted in the passage of over 600 trains during busy 24 hour periods. An unidentified Stanier loco drifts over towards the station in this Easterly view of the new viaduct. The immediate foreground is land which was once occupied by track serving Wellington Street Goods Depot (CLC).

28th MARCH 1968 ● P. SHACKCLOTH

Taken from an identical position as the top photograph, the driver of Edgeley's No **42354** leans well out of his cab for a clear sighting of the approaches to Edgeley Station. The signalman in Stockport No 2 box, meanwhile, has already returned the Up Slow to Platform 1 Signal to danger whilst the stock of the train continues to rumble over the viaduct.

1956 ● P. SHACKCLOTH COLLECTION

Although Longsight was generally regarded as a passenger depot, an interesting variety of mixed traffic and freight locos swelled the allocation over the years. Stanier 'Crab' 2-6-0 No **42979** was a 9A loco in the early 1950's and is pictured coming off the viaduct with a southbound goods train.   **c.1960** ● **A. BENDELL**

STOCKPORT
EDGELEY STATION

The Fowler Class 4P 2-6-4 Tanks were designed in 1927, primarily for heavier suburban services and were considered steady running, popular and reliable locos. They influenced the design of both Stanier and Fairburn versions which were soon to follow. Both Buxton and Macclesfield sheds had examples which passed through Stockport Edgeley on a daily basis with local commuter trains to and from Manchester London Road. Stockport's stud were used for a variety of duties, varying from local passenger to parcels and station pilot duties. No **42317** of Huddersfield Hillhouse is an unusual loco bringing in the afternoon service from Bradford.   **AUG 1965** ● **G. HARROP**

The same loco awaits departure from Platform 3A with the return working. **42317** was on Watford Junction's books during the 1950's and worked on duties to London Euston. Many of the trains ran non stop over the 17.5 miles with a 20 minute allowance. Speeds of up to 70mph and over were frequently recorded with early arrivals as a consequence. Upon transfer in 1959, it led a nomadic existence with brief spells at Springs Branch, Wigan (8F) and Carlisle Canal (12C) before Huddersfield from where it was withdrawn in 1965. It's doubtful whether the loco ever achieved such speeds wearing anything other than a 1C, Watford Junction shedplate.

AUG 1965 ● **G. HARROP**

LNWR DAYS

A rare glimpse of Edgeley station just after the turn of the century. A Dreadnought three cylinder compound Class 2-2-2-0 draws into Platform 2 with a London bound train. The *London and North Western Railway* driver offers a friendly wave to a colleague on the footplate of Ramsbottom 'DX' Class 0-6-0 waiting in the 'slums'. The stabled carriage is a 30' 1" brake third D361, built new in 1888 and possessing a dual braking system.

c.1905 ● P. SHACKCLOTH COLLECTION

Platform ticket issued 19th March 1960

A 'Super D' on passenger duty was an unusual occurrence. Originally introduced in 1912, the ex-LNWR 0-8-0's were a common sight over the years at Stockport Edgeley, plodding through with all manner of freight traffic. This rebuilt example, No **8903** (10C - Patricroft) unexpectedly arrived at the head of a Leigh - Buxton day excursion train. Fittingly, the train would probably have journeyed largely over ex-LNWR metals by way of Tyldesley, Eccles, Ordsall Lane, Manchester London Road (MSJ&A line) from where a path would be found on the main line to Stockport. Some eleven years after this photograph, and with the engine still on Patricroft's books, it was involved in a well documented disaster. On the damp and foggy day of December 11th 1947, the crew lost control whilst working an oil train from Neville Hill, Leeds to Eccles. The incident occurred on the notorious Miles Platting incline (1 in 47) on the eastern approaches to Manchester Victoria Station. The through lines were occupied and the signalmen at both Millgate and Turntable boxes had no alternative but to divert the runaway train into Bay Platform 7. It ploughed through the concourse before coming to rest. Incredibly, the engine suffered little damage and was towed away on her own wheels, a testament indeed to the ruggedness of Bowen-Cooke's original design. After repair it enjoyed a further two years in service and survived nationalisation yet never received its BR number. (4)8903 was finally withdrawn during October 1949. **19th JULY 1936 ● A. HAYNES COLLECTION**

L&YR VISITOR

Another visitor more familiar with the Miles Platting incline than Edgeley station was this *Lancashire and Yorkshire Railway* 2-4-2 Radial Tank. No **1526** was the first member of a final batch of 20 non-superheater engines introduced in 1910. Nos 1526 - 1531 were sent to Newton Heath to work on the semi-fast trains out of Manchester Victoria Station. The class, however, were daily visitors with one of the Colne contingent (Nos 1536 - 1540) arriving mid morning from that town with carriages for London. A white enamel plate within No 1526's cab roof would show '1', this being the shed code for Newton Heath which was easily the largest of the 32 depots on the L&YR system. Stockport Edgeley's shed code at the time was 16S falling within the LNWR Longsight (Manchester) District. It became 9B in 1935, midway through the LMS period (1923 - 1948), at which time Newton Heath was re-coded 26A.

c.1912 ● E. MASON

Although **Stockport Edgeley** was the larger, more important of the town's two main stations, this was hardly reflected in their architectural styles. Tiviot Dale was a grand affair and had an ecclesiastical air whilst the less convenient Edgeley had a more austere feel. Two roads flanked by imposing retaining walls offered the rail user a choice of approach. The more commonly used easterly side was nearer the town whilst Edgeley and Shaw Heath were served from the west. A dank and dismal subway connected these approaches and acted as the station entrance. Free platform tickets were issued at either end which, in turn, were exchanged for travel tickets purchased from booking offices situated on both Up and Down platforms. Such a duplication of manpower would hardly be tolerated today.

28th MAY 1960 ● **G. WHITEHEAD**

STOCKPORT EDGELEY STATION

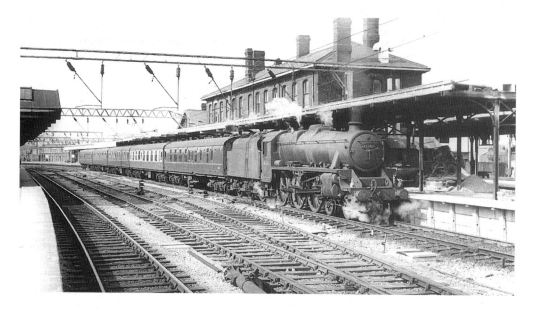

Stanier Class Five 4-6-0 No 45310 of Bushbury shed (21C), awaits departure from Platform 2 with a semi-fast train for Birmingham New Street. At this time, parts of the station were in the throes of refurbishment with the new Up platform canopy in situ. Note the contrasting original version on the Down platform to the left of the view. The original station opened here on 15th February 1843.

28th MAY 1960 ●
G. WHITEHEAD

The south end of the Up platforms. The single line bay between Platforms 1 and 2 was rarely used. The immediate post-war period, however, saw a schools train departing at 4.15pm which called at all stations to Alderley Edge. After electrification, the standby loco could often be found there. Framed in the canopy stanchions, a Midland 3F 0-6-0 visiting from Gorton, No **43330,** is at work in the coal yard whilst to the far right, in Vernon Sidings, a train of conflats is assembled from the gantry straddling the tracks. This will form the nightly run to London Broad Street, departing at 11.08pm, and was regarded as one of Edgeley MPD's top link duties. Note the station totem, 'Stockport Edgeley' hanging at a jaunty angle! One assumes it survived this phase of the upgrade.

28th MAY 1960 ● **G. WHITEHEAD**

With the closure of Tiviot Dale on 2nd January 1967, the need to differentiate between the town's stations was no longer necessary. Consequently Stockport Edgeley was simply renamed 'Stockport', without ceremony, on 19th March 1967. The short lived signs which replaced the totems await removal from the platforms.

21st MARCH 1967 ● **P. SHACKCLOTH**

EDGELEY'S JUBILEES

By the early 1960s, many of the Class 6P Jubilee 4-6-0s became surplus to requirements on the main line as dieselisation took a stranglehold on the majority of express passenger duties. As a consequence, some gravitated to the less glamorous, predominately freight depots such as Stockport Edgeley. In July 1962 Nos **45596 Bahamas** and **45632 Tonga** arrived from Carlisle (Upperby) and were put to work on more mundane work. A further four members of the class were allocated for short periods but these two were in residence together for three years before *Tonga* took off to Newton Heath in August 1965 to see out another two months in service. 9B's sole surviving 'Jub', the double-chimneyed Bahamas, soldiered on, becoming the pride and joy of the shed staff. She was kept in excellent condition and eventually became the subject of an on-off preservation attempt. After a long period of storage, the loco - now officially condemned, was dragged out to form part of a cavalcade of locos bound for Crewe Works and oblivion. An eleventh hour telephone call saw her quickly detached and returned to the safety of the back of number six road. The rest, as they say, is history.

(ABOVE) **Nose to nose.** At rest in the shed yard. Both are in light steam and await their next duties. JANUARY 1965 ● P. JORDAN

(BELOW) **No 45632 Tonga** stands on number eight road ready to move off shed and work an excursion train. The class, designed by Stanier, were noted for their hard working qualities and many trips had speeds in excess of 80mph being recorded. JUNE 1965 ● G. HARROP

VISITING LOCOS

Fowler Class 7F 0-8-0 No 49515. *26A - Newton Heath*

c.1959 ● P. SHACKCLOTH COLLECTION

Riddles WD Class 2-8-0 No 90586. *50B - Hull Dairycoates*

26th OCTOBER 1965 ● G. HARROP

Standard Class 5 4-6-0 No 73171. *55D - Royston*

10th JANUARY 1963 ● J. PEDEN

Ex 'Franco-Crosti' Class 9F 2-10-0 No 92020. *8H - Birkenhead*

13th JUNE 1966 ● G. HARROP

Britannia Class 7P 4-6-2 No 70038 *Robin Hood*. *12A - Carlisle Kingmoor*

1st JULY 1967 ● P. JORDAN

STOCKPORT COUNTY FOOTBALL CLUB

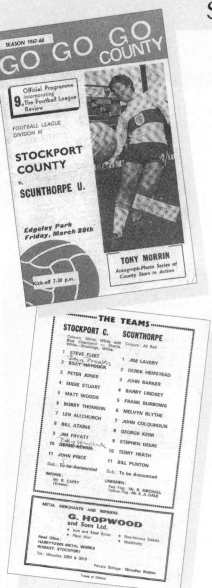

*For the record, County won the game 4 - 1
with goals by Johnny Price, Bill Atkins (2)
and Bill Fryatt. The attendance was 6,779.*

Edgeley Park, home of Stockport County Football Club, bordered onto Edgeley shed yard. A group of spotters-cum-County fans regularly gathered beside the tea hut from where it was possible to observe engine movements whilst keeping an eye on the match. County were one of the first clubs to introduce Friday night football rather than compete on Saturdays with their more illustrious neighbours, Manchester's City and United. Original floodlights had been installed in 1956 but were under utilised. The decision proved popular and their new 'Go Go Go' image regularly attracted crowds of up to 10,000. The referees' whistle was constantly punctuated by those of Stanier Class 5's and 8F's and another hazard was the pall of smoke which would drift over if the wind was in the wrong direction! After the game, many of the gathering would then do a quick bunk round the shed before retiring to the Nelson Hotel. It was on such an occasion that these photos were taken.

29th MARCH 1968 ● P. SHACKCLOTH

INSIDE 9B

Two examples of locos of Fowler's design stand side by side in the depths of the shed. 2-6-4 Tank No **42424** was the last member of a class of 125 engines. The final 30 to be built were fitted with side windowed cabs. Together with three other latter examples, 42424 enjoyed a lengthy spell allocated to Tebay specifically for banking the heavier northbound trains up to Shap summit on the West Coast Main Line. No **42793** was a member of the 'Crab' Class 2-6-0 based for many years some 25 miles further north at Carlisle Kingmoor (12A). Although of reasonably close proximity, it is unlikely that these two locos' paths would have regularly crossed. Kingmoor was largely responsible for workings to the north into Scotland over the ex-Caledonian and Glasgow & South Western routes and to the south by way of the picturesque Settle & Carlisle route. Carlisle Upperby (12B) duties tended to be to the south on the West Coast Main line. When Upperby closed to steam on 12th December 1966, Kingmoor's engines were more in evidence over Shap but by this time both the 'Crab' and Fowler tank classes were extinct. No 42424 was a 9B loco for 17 months, being withdrawn in September 1964 whilst No 42793 saw the year out, having been on Edgeley's books a mere nine months.

13th SEPT 1964 ● G. HARROP

Driver Eric Bailey approaches with oil can in hand about to prepare one of the depot's Class Fives, No **44940** for the road. The loco had been recently cleaned at the bottom of No 2 road near the foreman's office in readiness for a special working.

10th DECEMBER 1967 ● P. SHACKCLOTH

A shed labourer has the unpleasant task of removing ash and clinker from one of the pits within the depot whilst stabled alongside is another of the Edgeley contingent of Stanier Class 5's, No **45200** undergoing a routine boiler washout.

10th DECEMBER 1967 ● P. SHACKCLOTH

Jubilees are considered by many to be Stanier's most attractive design. Their pleasing lines are shown off to good effect in this study of No **45580** *Burma* awaiting its next duty behind Edgeley shed. The loco was a long time resident of Blackpool (24E) before transfer to Warrington Dallam in June 1963 and this visit was possibly one of its final duties as an 8B loco. The name and numberplate remain 'in situ', the latter secured by a single bolt! When transferred to Newton Heath later in September 1964 for a final three months' stint in service, it arrived bereft of these items, removed by officialdom who were becoming increasingly conscious of their market value.

13th SEPTEMBER 1964 ● **G. HARROP**

VISITING LOCOS

One of the Edgeley favourites, Fowler 2-6-4T No **42343,** a loco kept in clean condition, rubs shoulders with a grubby Jubilee 6P 4-6-0 No **45590** *Travancore* visiting from Newton Heath Depot. During the 1960's many locos moved from depot to depot for no apparent reason, especially to the enthusiast. This example had arrived from nearby Agecroft in June 1963, but some three months later had moved on to Warrington Dallam. In the meantime the loco correctly sported a 26A shedplate.

JULY 1963 ● **G. HARROP**

Standard Class 4 4-6-0 No 75054, in typically forlorn condition, stands in the shed yard buffered up to a Stanier 8F 2-8-0. This mixed traffic loco was built at Swindon Works before entering service at Chester (Midland) depot in December 1956. After a spell 'down the road' at Mold Junction, it moved on to Bletchley before taking up final residence at Stoke depot. Many of the class gravitated to 5D in the latter years and became regular visitors to Edgeley. Once again, this was possibly the loco's final visit as it was withdrawn some 5 weeks later.

26th JUNE 1966 ● **G. HARROP**

BR Britannia Pacific No 70013 *Oliver Cromwell* paid two visits to the depot during April 1968 in association with railtours. She was the surviving member of the class left in service which were perhaps best remembered for their sterling work on the 2 hour London Liverpool Street - Norwich expresses. No 70013 went new to Norwich in June 1951 and spent a decade there before moving on to March, Carlisle Kingmoor, Upperby and Kingmoor again before taking up final residence at Carnforth in 1968. Happily the loco survives in preservation.

28th APRIL 1968 ● T. RENSHAW

On the morning of Friday, 5th March 1966, midway through a life drawing class at Stockport College, the author was made aware of a rumour circulating that a rare bird had been spotted down the road in Edgeley. Such a rare bird was justification for the Head of Department to grant permission for the whole class to immediately go and observe this stranger. As a consequence, a mass exodus of art students descended on Edgeley shed to view Gresley A4 Pacific **No 60019** *Bittern.* The loco had arrived light engine prior to working a railtour from Manchester Piccadilly to Derby via Crewe and Stoke two days later. Despite the unofficial visit, the shed authorities made the students most welcome, being proud to show off such a prestigious visitor.

5th MARCH 1966 ● P. SHACKCLOTH

Another ex-LNER visitor was K4 2-6-0 No 3442 *The Great Marquess.* She worked into Stockport with a railtour entitled 'The Mercian' and is standing on the reception road. A shed labourer attends to matters and is caught leaning precariously over the ash pit in the process. 3442 was resplendent in original LNER apple green livery and the red buffer beam carried details of loco number, class and home depot (Leeds, Neville Hill). The loco was one of only six introduced in 1937 specifically for work on the West Highland Line. She carried No 61994 in BR days and worked mainly out of Eastfield (Glasgow) depot. *The Great Marquess* was an early candidate for preservation and was purchased by Viscount Garnock in 1961.

5th APRIL 1967 ● P. SHACKCLOTH COLLECTION

Further variety arrived from the south in the form of Class MN 'Merchant Navy' Pacific No **35026** *Lamport & Holt Line.* The following day the loco worked a circular railtour from Manchester Piccadilly to York, returning to Victoria, which was organised by 'Williams Deacons Bank Club', members of whom were instrumental in the survival of Jubilee No 45596 *Bahamas.*

19th NOVEMBER 1966 ● G. HARROP

A Longsight 'Royal Scot' No 46115 *Scots Guardsman* ambles off shed prior to heading an excursion. Over the years, Edgeley played host to a multitude of locos from distant sheds.

A couple of examples were:
Standard Class Five 4-6-0 No 73087 (82F) Bath (Green Park) - *21st August 1960.*
ex LNER V2 2-6-2 No 60842 (50A) York *24th September 1960.*

12th JUNE 1963 ● **R. BLENCOWE**

Relegated to lowly freight duties and working out of Farnley Junction Depot, it is hard to believe that within a year Jubilee 4-6-0 No **45562** *Alberta* would have the honour of hauling the last steam worked Royal Train on BR. On 30th May 1967, The Duke of Edinburgh travelled behind the loco from York whilst en route to Harrogate. By now *Alberta* had become a high profile loco as one of only five remaining members of this distinguished class, all now based at Leeds Holbeck Depot. They were cherished by a band of dedicated enthusiasts who made weekly pilgrimages there to keep them in pristine condition during their final hours.

4th JULY 1966 ● **G. HARROP**

A double header bound for London gets into its stride from Stockport and is seen passing Edgeley shed. The impressive combination are a pair of Longsight locomotives, both in excellent external condition. The 'pilot' is Stanier Class 5 No **44937**, one of 14 such locos that sported 9A plates at the time, whilst the 'train' engine is Britannia Pacific No **70032** *Tennyson*. Longsight took delivery of several 'Brits' during the 1950's to augment its Class 7P motive power but never had any 'Duchesses' on its books. Unfortunately the Class 8P locos were prohibited from running over the direct line to London, via Stoke at the time. Standing majestically in the background is 'Our Lady's R.C. Church, situated on Shaw Heath. **MAY 1958** ● **P. SHACKCLOTH COLLECTION**

During December 1963, six withdrawn ex-GWR locos paused en-route from Salop to Sheffield for scrapping. They were 4-6-0 'County' Class Nos 1017 *County of Hereford*, No 1022 *County of Northampton* and No 1026 *County of Salop*, 4-6-0 'Castle' Class No 5015 *Kingswear Castle* and 2-6-0 Moguls Nos **7309** (pictured) and 7336. Stanier Class 5 No 44755 with Caprotti valve gear was also part of the cavalcade.　**15th DECEMBER 1963 ● G. HARROP**

Another loco destined for the scrapyard was Stanier Class 3 2-6-2T No **40147**. It was withdrawn from Wakefield depot and although now bereft of a 56A shedplate, the loco rather surprisingly still carries its front numberplate. The original British Railways 'lion and wheel' totem unusually remains in evidence on the tank side.

15th DECEMBER 1963 ● G. HARROP

WITHDRAWN FROM SERVICE

Withdrawn locos from both Stockport Edgeley and Heaton Mersey Depots were often held in the Sand Sidings, pending their final journeys to the scrapyard. This elevated view from Stockholm Road features Stanier Class 5's and 8F's standing in isolation. Nearest to the camera is No **44940** which has turned its last wheel in active service. Cylinder head covers and parts of the motion have been placed on the frames. The red buffer beam suggests that it had received attention prior to withdrawal, presumably for a special working, although the tender seemingly didn't!

19th APRIL 1968 ● G. HARROP

The only locomotive to be cut up in Stockport was Stanier Class 5 4-6-0 No **45249**. The records show that it was disposed of by T. Ward & Co of Sheffield in the Sand Sidings behind Edgeley Depot as it was unfit to travel to the breakers yard. The loco was reduced to 75 tons of scrap metal within two days. The non ferrous types were the main attraction and the copper content within the firebox could realise up to £500 per ton. Brass valves and cab fittings also had a value and were often pilfered immediately upon a loco's withdrawal.　**12th JUNE 1967 ● G. HARROP**

IMAGES AT EDGELEY SHED

1968 ● P. SHACKCLOTH

EDGELEY JUNCTION

In the early 1950's, Longsight had an impressive stud of Class 6 and 7 motive power. In addition to the newly delivered Britannias and the older Patriots and Royal Scots, it had a dozen or so Jubilees all of which worked regularly through Stockport with services in and out of Manchester London Road Station. One of these, No **45556 Nova Scotia** gets into its stride with an Up express bound for London Euston. Edgeley Junction No 1 signal box, seen above the second carriage, controlled amongst other things, the ex-LNWR timber bracket home signal. This stood some 70ft tall and dominated the local scene. Beyond the busy Edgeley Marshalling Yard is the branch to Cheadle and Northenden Junction whilst the line to Buxton trails away to the right.

c.1953 ● J. DAVENPORT

A returning empty oil train bound for Stanlow gets away in dramatic style from Edgeley Junction. It will travel via Northenden Junction before heading through Warrington towards Helsby and Stanlow. 9F 2-10-0 No **92094**, one of the large batch allocated to Birkenhead, looks in poor condition with evidence of heavy priming around the boiler. The crudely applied front number and shed code typified many examples of remaining locos of all classes in the last few years of steam. The standby loco, a Type A electric Bo-Bo is tucked away in the coal yard to the right whilst the Down line may well be 'In Possession', occupied by two engineers' vans standing opposite Edgeley Junction No 1 signal box.

7th OCTOBER 1967 ● G. HARROP

ADSWOOD

A Webb Coal Engine 0-6-0 No 8278 drifts past Adswood Sidings with a lengthy mixed goods train. This view looking south towards Cheadle Hulme is from Siddington Road bridge. Adswood Road disappears away to the left, but a local landmark, the 'Wembley Hotel' is just out of view further down. Stockport was the relieving point for much of the freight traffic from the Crewe direction. Locos were often re-manned by Edgeley crews alongside the depot to work forward, very often into Yorkshire for which they knew the road.

MAY 1936 ● W. POTTER

Fowler 2-6-4T No 2379 approaches Adswood Road Up Main Distant signal with a stopping train to Crewe. The other signal just in view is Adswood Road Up Goods Distant which was permanently fixed at caution, as this particular line converged at Adswood Road leaving only the Up and Down main lines to cross Ladybridge Viaduct, just beyond the Borough boundary. Looking in the Stockport direction, this photograph is also taken from Siddington Road bridge. The nearer of the other two bridges behind the train carries the ex-LNWR 'Stockport Junction' Line between Cheadle Village Junction and Davenport Junction, commonly referred to as the 'Khyber'. That beyond is Stockholm Road bridge whilst the imposing signal at Edgeley Junction, referred to on the opposite page, is also clearly visible.

MARCH 1948 ● T. LEWIS

Another view from the same location and another Fowler 2-6-4 tank. No **2397** approaches Edgeley Junction on the Down main sporting express passenger head-lamps. The five coaches are all of Stanier corridor stock which suggests that the train has split at Crewe with the other portion bound for Liverpool. Behind the loco, the fledgling Bridge Hall Estate is under course of construction. The ex-LNWR water tank which stood at the throat of Adswood Sidings, was removed in connection with the Manchester to Crewe electrification scheme.

MARCH 1948 ● T. LEWIS

The same loco in BR days. The driver of **No 42397,** running bunker first, has clear signals from Adswood Road box to proceed towards Cheadle Hulme with a local train to Macclesfield. A pall of smoke hangs over Adswood Sidings and Bridge Hall Estate in the loco's wake. Prominent fishplates on the Permanent Way suggest that the oiling gang had recently attended to this section in readiness for the summer months.

31st MAY 1954 ● T. LEWIS

Adswood Sidings Covered Ground Frame controlled traffic in and out of the sidings from the Down goods lines only. This LMS standard pattern structure was somewhat unusual as it featured ornamental ridge tiles. The main lines pass behind the building.

15th MARCH 1967 ● P. SHACKCLOTH

It is interesting to compare this photograph with those on the previous page. Gone are the water tank and semaphore signals, replaced by masts and catenary necessary for the Manchester - Crewe electrification scheme. BR also appears to have claimed land over the years as the kink in the fencing testifies. The double garage with its attractive gable end remains in situ although the property immediately behind has disappeared. An unidentified electric 'A' Class loco approaches from the south with a lengthy van train whilst Stanier Class Five No **44818** marshals more vans in the sidings. A nice touch, though, is the recently planted sapling, supported by a stake.

15th MARCH 1967 ● P. SHACKCLOTH

ADSWOOD SIDINGS

Another view of the sidings with Stanier Class 5 No **44818** about to retire to nearby Edgeley shed for servicing. One of 9B's three BR Diesel Shunters, No **D3769** is also in view. The ramshackle affair between the locos is a concrete sectional hut with modifications by the shunting staff. The fire devil, which was designed to prevent water columns from freezing in the depths of winter, has been put to good use as an impromptu brazier. There appears to be no shortage of fuel in the vicinity!

15th MARCH 1967 ● P. SHACKCLOTH

This was the spot that acted like a magnet to the more intrepid trainspotter. It was somewhat akin to the celebrated farmer's field south of Rugby Station which afforded views of the West Coast Main line in conjunction with the Great Central which crossed on a lattice bridge at high level. A constant procession of trains were witnessed there, and it was much the same here - at 'Cross Bridges', where the ex-LNWR main line from Manchester London Road Station to the south crossed over the ex-Midland main line which ran out of Manchester's Central Station. Another member of the Longsight family of 'Royal Scot' 4-6-0's, No **46111** *Royal Fusilier* gets into her stride with a southbound express. Adswood Sidings are away to the left.

7th NOVEMBER 1954 ● T. LEWIS

DAVENPORT STATION

(ABOVE) **A bitterly cold morning in February 1955** witnesses Fowler 2-6-4T No **42371** about to depart with a Manchester London Road to Buxton local train. The carriages appear to be thoroughly steam heated but the recent snowfall fails to distinguish the Up platform edge from the permanent way. In days gone by, Station Masters would detail porters to keep the platforms clear. Conditions such as these were a contributory factor regarding the line's survival, Buxton being often only accessible by rail. The Fowler Tanks were the mainstay of this service for many years and this one spent its entire working life operating out of Buxton (9D) shed, being delivered there new on 19th September 1929.

15th FEBRUARY 1955 ● D. R. MORGAN

(ABOVE) **Looking towards Hazel Grove,** this low level view illustrates the neat and tidy appearance of the first station out of Stockport on the Buxton Branch. Note the tree stump seemingly growing out of the Down platform building roof which has recently received attention from a surgeon. The trusty Fowler Tanks and their suburban stock were eventually replaced by Diesel Multiple Units on 26th September 1960.

15th JUNE 1966 ● G. HARROP

(RIGHT) **When Stockport County** were drawn to play mighty Liverpool away in the FA Cup, special trains were laid on for the fans' big day out. Stanier Class Five No **45382** is seen at Woodsmoor Crossing prior to working one of these trains, starting out from Hazel Grove.

30th JANUARY 1965 ● G. HARROP

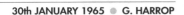

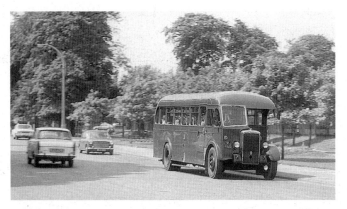

A Salford Corporation welfare bus is caught on camera passing Woodsmoor Lane, heading south down the A6. The vehicle, No 450 (CRJ 450) is a Daimler CVG6 with Burlingham bodywork and may well be on its way to Lyme Park on a Sunday day trip. Introduced in 1950, its previous regular haunts were Service No 4 between Prestwich and Simister village and Service No 5 which ran from Victoria Bus Station (Salford) to Peel Green, passing under the notorious Barton Aqueduct.

21st JUNE 1969 ● R. KEELEY

BUS VARIETY

A series of three photographs all taken at the same location on Woodsmoor Lane near the junction with Flowery Field. They nicely illustrate the different models within the Stockport Corporation fleet, all working Service No 23 between Stockport Mersey Square and Woodsmoor (Crossway). ● R. KEELEY

(TOP RIGHT) Crossley DD42/5 No 247 (CJA 771) one of the later series built in 1948 with H30/26R Crossley bodywork. JUNE 1965

(CENTRE) Leyland Titan PD2/30 No 351 (PJA 921) built in 1960 with H32/28R Longwell Green bodywork. JULY 1967

(BELOW) Leyland Titan PD3/14 No 93 (MJA 893G) built in 1969 with H38/32F East Lancs forward entrance bodywork. This was one of the Corporation's last vehicles to be delivered before the services were taken over by SELNEC later in 1969. JUNE 1969

Traffic on the A6 between Stockport and Hazel Grove has remained a problem for many years. This view, looking towards Great Moor, shows the great diversity of road transport of the day. Sandwiched between three North Western buses travelling south towards Hazel Grove is a Stockport Corporation Crossley DD 42/3 (one of the first batch: 207/225-244). The bus has arrived at Stepping Hill on Service No 16 and is about to turn left into Dialstone Lane to commence its return journey to Stockport only - the full service ran to Chorlton. 1960 ● D. GILL

Facilities at Bredbury Junction were primitive. Coal and water were dropped off by the Brinnington banker as required to the 18 lever signalbox which was devoid of electricity. This view from the box taken in the depths of winter records Heaton Mersey ex-LMS 4F 0-6-0 No **44250** running down the gradient with a mixed bag of wagons. The tall CLC lattice signals were a feature of the area to assist enginemens' visibility. That behind the loco protects the 'Marple Curve', whose lines climb away to meet the ex-Great Central and Midland joint line at Romiley Junction. The rear of the train is passing under a short viaduct which carried the line towards Belle Vue and Ashburys Junction. **5th JANUARY 1963 ● G. COLTAS**

Eastbound trains passing through Tiviot Dale Station were immediately faced with an arduous climb through Brinnington and Bredbury. Stanier 8F 2-8-0 No **48161**, in surprisingly clean condition for a Heaton Mersey loco, bursts clear of the 168 yard long Brinnington tunnel with mineral empties. The brilliant sunshine nicely highlights the radiating stone portal at the mouth and the retaining wall which fell away in ledges. The loco carries a star on the cab side indicating that it was a member of the class which had the balancing of its moving parts improved. This enabled running speeds at faster than 40 mph which encompassed passenger work on occasions.

9th JUNE 1962 ● G. COLTAS

BRINNINGTON TUNNEL

Looking west over the Mersey Valley beyond which lay the suburbs of South Reddish, an unidentified Stanier 8F 2-8-0 slogs up the gradient blackening the Brinnington sky in the process, on the western approach to the tunnel. The empty mineral wagons will pass Bredbury, Woodley and Apethorne Junctions before reaching the interchange sidings at Brookfold, Godley Junction - the eastern extremity of the CLC system. At this point steam gave way to electric traction for the onward journey over the Pennines via Woodhead en route to the Yorkshire coalfield. Brookfold provided both turntable and watering facilities for steam locos which were predominantly based at Heaton Mersey and Speke Junction (Garston) depots.

1967 ● E. HUMPHREY

The 6.45pm Manchester Central to Chinley/ Sheffield Midland stopping train gets into its stride away from Tiviot Dale Station and passes through Portwood behind Fowler 2-6-4T No **42306** (9D - Buxton). The imposing goods warehouse lies behind the rear coaches opposite which are the coal sidings and yard. Mottram Street lies beneath the first carriage and the wide bridge here carries some 8 running lines.

4th MAY 1962 ● G. COLTAS

The architectural splendour of Tiviot Dale Station rather eclipsed that of its busier, more important counterpart, Edgeley. Whilst the Jacobean facade had an ecclesiastical air and the stone setts formed an impressive forecourt, the interior was dark, dank and foreboding. It served the travelling public between 1st December 1865 and 1st January 1967, being demolished six months later.

7th NOVEMBER 1964 ● G. HARROP

An interesting class of loco arrived at Heaton Mersey in 1959 when the depot took delivery of three Standard BR Class 4 2-6-0's. Nos 76085 & 76087 arrived from Saltley in January and were joined by No **76048** from Skipton in May. The latter has worked the 4.56pm stopping train from Liverpool Central to Stockport Tiviot Dale arriving at 6.34pm. An unidentified 'Derby 4' 0-6-0 stands in the bay platform between banking durties.

23rd JUNE 1962 ● G. COLTAS

Two young trainspotters diligently record the passage of Fowler 0-6-0 No **44456** returning to Heaton Mersey depot. The banking loco on this occasion was Fairburn 2-6-4T No **42159** which had little or no local passenger work by this time. The soot-ridden footbridge connecting Up and Down platforms was unique. Smoke penetrated loose floorboards and many a passenger creaked over this bridge through a fog of smoke. The photograph was taken from a similar vantage point to that above two years later. Note the high rise flats which now dominate the skyline beyond Lancashire Hill.

7th NOVEMBER 1964 ● G. HARROP

Yet another class of loco is observed here engaged on Brinnington banking duties. These mixed traffic Moguls were introduced in 1947 by H.G.Ivatt and were nicknamed 'Flying Pigs'. They were hardly the most attractive of locos but were eminently functional with high running plate which offered easier access for servicing. With steam leaking from many joints, No **43063** idles the time away before the passage of the next train requiring assistance. The platform seat has been so positioned by the locomen for their own benefit.

2nd APRIL 1964 ● G. WHITEHEAD

ᴇ STATION

On the approach to Tiviot Dale Station from the east, the line crosses numerous bridges and short viaducts in the Portwood area. A Robinson 04 2-8-0 No **63767** drifts light engine over the bridge beneath which flows the River Tame. The confluence of the Tame and Goyt at this point create the source of the River Mersey

5th DECEMBER 1960 ● G. COLTAS

The ex CLC main line continued to handle a considerable volume of freight traffic after the closure of the station. The most common class of loco in the latter years were the Stanier 8F 2-8-0's. Clearly identified on the buffer beam as a Trafford Park member, No **48356** brings a Godley Junction to Northwich train made up of 'Presflo' cement wagons through the middle road. These wagons will strike a chord with those enthusiasts who also tried their hand at railway modelling. It was one of a number of popular 'Airfix' 00 gauge plastic kits available from the early 1960's.

7th NOVEMBER 1967 ● P. SHACKCLOTH

Gorton shed had regular workings over the CLC using their large stud of 04 2-8-0's for many years. After withdrawal in 1962, the WD 2-8-0's became commonplace. Unkempt No **90010** soldiers on with a mixed goods. Note the Midland style platform seat with wrought iron front leg missing. It carries the name 'Stockport', in common with the signal box which was previously 'Stockport Tiviot Dale East'. The Alligator Mill in the background became one of seven 19th century buildings which once formed the Bee Hive complex. Despite suffering a serious fire in 1980, the shell survived for a further 15 years.

7th NOVEMBER 1964 ● G. HARROP

RAILTOUR DUTY

The Manchester University Railway Society organised an excursion encompassing a 150 mile round trip through Cheshire and the Potteries. It was scheduled to depart from the former Midland Railway's goods depot at Ancoats, Manchester and the selected loco was Fowler 2-6-4T No **42343,** one of the last of its class remaining in service and immaculately turned out by Stockport Edgeley depot. The train consisted of five ex LMS open vestibule vehicles of which two were brake seconds. The 'Staffordshire Potter' is passing through the station at 11.0am, already 30 minutes behind schedule. The crew were Driver Arthur Walker and Fireman Ted Whitham, both Gorton men, who are probably working one of that depot's last passenger turns - 9G closed two months later. The route was via Northwich, Stoke, Congleton, Cauldon Quarry, Stoke and Bollington before returning to Ancoats.

13th MARCH 1965 ● P. FITTON

Hanover Congregational Chapel dominates this view looking east over the Portwood district of Stockport. Originally built in 1821, it was demolished in 1966, shortly before Tiviot Dale Station station itself. The train of vans is standing in one of the two bay platforms from where local services to Woodley and Romiley and to Manchester London Road via Reddish once ran. The Georgian courts of houses, off Lancashire Hill and to the left of the Chapel, looked down on to the two-road Tiviot Dale Engine Shed which closed upon the opening of Heaton Mersey in January 1889. The building was demolished and turntable later removed, but the water tank and some original track remained in situ until the very end. By the early 1960's, many of the cotton mills in view were empty and derelict. The 'green giant' gasometer remained prominent though, although a great number of terraced rows within its shadow had been swept away.

30th MAY 1963 ● STOCKPORT EXPRESS

The line between Tiviot Dale Station and Georges Road is a combination of cuttings, short tunnels and bridges. Stanier 8F 2-8-0 No **48684** (9F) brings mineral empties towards Wellington Street Tunnel on the approaches to Georges Road. Immediately behind the photographer was a set of run back catch points on the Down line, protecting the short 1 in 74 gradient through the tunnel. On a severe frosty night during the winter of 1960, the rear section of a train similar to this, a Heaton Mersey bound freight, parted company after being held at a stand on the incline for a period of time. The resultant run back diverted the ex-LMS guards van and wagons at the catch point into the solid sandstone wall, seen to the right of the 8F. The Gorton breakdown gang removed the concertinaed wagons the following day but when the brake van was finally recovered, its tail lamp was squashed perfectly flat, embedded in the wall. The force of impact was obvious but the guard remained injury free, having jumped well clear beforehand. The wreckage was transported to the sidings behind Tiviot Dale Station before being cut up and loaded into wagons.

11th FEBRUARY 1967 ● B. CRICK

WELLINGTON STREET TUNNEL

When the 9F's began to congregate in great numbers at Birkenhead and Speke Junction depots during 1965, they became regular visitors to the town, working on both major routes with traffic from Merseyside bound mainly for Yorkshire. Although Stockport Edgeley and Heaton Mersey serviced the class, neither depot had any on their own allocation, nor indeed, did any of the 733 strong WD 2-8-0 locos carry 9B or 9F shedplates either. Designed by Riddles and introduced in 1954, the Class 9F 2-10-0 eventually numbered 251 locos, but by 1st January 1968 there remained a mere 18 in service, based only at Speke Junction (8C) and Carnforth (10A) Depots. The fireman of No 92218 (8C), leaning well out of his cab, is no doubt anxious to catch an early sight of the Tiviot Dale Outer Home signal as he plunges into the short Wellington Street Tunnel with an eastbound mixed goods train. The loco was withdrawn two months later, having spent just over eight years on revenue earning service for BR. What a waste! Meanwhile, high above on the viaduct, wagons from a Stanlow - Leeds oil train, hauled by a Stanier 8F 2-8-0 pass by. Had it arrived 30 seconds or so earlier, it would have made for one of those unique photographs with both engines in view.

28th MARCH 1968 ● P. SHACKCLOTH

GEORGES ROAD

Georges Road Junction Signalbox. To the right of the box are Georges Road Sidings, beyond which is the embankment carrying the electrified main line from Manchester Piccadilly to Crewe. The distinctive Marples Furniture Stores building stands on the horizon. Heaton Norris Station lay immediately behind the box itself, whilst the spire of St Thomas's Church may be glimpsed behind the lower signal arm. The underbridge at the top end of Georges Road, carrying the main line, had a severe height restriction and more than one Corporation bus came to grief as a consequence over the years.

25th SEPTEMBER 1966 ● G. HARROP

Georges Road Bridge bisected two groups of sidings and was witness to intense weekday shunting activitities. A Trafford Park Class Five, No **45150** is signalled into Club House from Georges Road and is about to cross the bridge. Such duties warranted a target engine from nearby Heaton Mersey shed who regularly provided a 'Derby 4', but towards the end of steam, larger locos were available for such mundane tasks. This particular loco's claim to fame was that it handled the final 5.22pm Manchester Central - Buxton on Friday 3rd March 1967. This had latterly been in the hands of Jubilee No 45705 *Seahorse*, a popular choice amongst the spotting fraternity. Meanwhile an ex-Crosti boilered 2-10-0, No **92025** approaches on the Up main line with eastbound mineral empties. **28th FEBRUARY 1966 ● G. COLTAS**

A returning Llandudno - Nottingham relief train heads south down the Midland main line with Stanier Class Five No **45032** in charge of an interesting assortment of coaching stock. This loco, somewhat surprisingly, was on Warrington Dallam's (8B) books and would have journeyed through its home town, then via Lymm and Broadheath before reaching Skelton, Northenden and Cheadle Junctions. Later in the day it will represent a 'cop' for many of the trainspotters gathered on both Derby and Nottingham Midland Stations, although many would have wished for a 'Western Lines' Jubilee instead.

c.1952 ● B.K.B. GREEN

ADSWOOD

The highly successful LMS Stanier designed freight loco, the 8F 2-8-0, was introduced in 1935 before being requisitioned by the War Department. As a consequence, the SR, LNER and GWR workshops also built examples, but by Nationalisation in 1948, the vast majority of the 663 strong class were based at ex-LMS depots. A fully laden, wooden bodied coal train rattles downgrade towards Cheadle Heath behind Stanier 8F No **8314.** Through the morning mists stand a variety of wagons and brake vans occupying the westernmost line within Adswood Sidings.

29th OCTOBER 1948 ● T. LEWIS

The 9.35am Blackpool North - Nottingham Midland approaches 'Cross Bridges' with a Burton (17B) 'Crab' 2-6-0 No **42799** in charge. An overbridge carrying the ex-LNWR main line south is situated immediately beyond Adswood Sidings. The climb over the Peak started in earnest over this section at 1 in 100 but the 9-coach excursion should pose few problems for the crew of this trusty workhorse. The photograph is taken from Adswood footbridge whilst another lattice version under the seventh carriage is Lark Mill. Just discernable in the background are the works of The Oil Well Engineering Company which bordered on to the extensive site of Henry Simon.

28th JULY 1951 ● J. DAVENPORT

Peace and tranquility. An unusual view looking north showing the Midland main line at a point between Cross Bridges, Adswood and Bramhall Moor Lane. A short goods train is making its way to Gowhole Sidings with an unidentified Robinson J10 0-6-0 in charge. This would have been one of Heaton Mersey's locos which were used on the daily pick up goods at this time. Davenport golf course lies behind the train, beyond which, in the far distance, is Cale Green Park, next to which are the grounds of Stockport Cricket Club whose boundary borders on the ex-LNWR Buxton branch between Davenport Junction and Davenport Station.

10th SEPTEMBER 1958 ● D.R. MORGAN

BRAMHALL MOOR LANE

A low winter's sun nicely captures the wheels and motion of Ivatt Class 2 2-6-0 No **43010** not long out of Horwich Works. Initially the class were fitted with unsightly double chimneys but were modified with single versions as they became due for overhaul. The short lived 'British Railways' appears on a tender which was designed to aid visibility when running in reverse, as in this case. The train consists of a motley collection of empty wooden bodied mineral wagons, the fourth of which is designed to carry coke. It is passing under Bramhall Moor Lane en route to Gowhole sidings.

2nd JANUARY 1952 ● T. LEWIS

The hopper trains continue to ply their trade between Tunstead Quarry and Wallerscote Sidings, Northwich. They were entrusted to the ubiquitous Stanier 8F 2-8-0's soon after their introduction in 1935 and the latter continued to give yeoman service until March 1968. Some of the hopper wagons were also of a similar vintage. A Heaton Mersey example is unusually employed on one of the workings which by this time were the pre-serve of Northwich locos. Before Nationalisation, Heaton Mersey engines and men had regular work on the 'Hoppers', but they did not complete the round trip. Operating either side of Cheadle Heath, the locomotives would change there and one set of men would work to Tunstead whilst another went to Northwich where a longer turn round was necessary. No **48127** returns a rake of 16 original empty hoppers en-route to Tunstead and is about to pass under the bridge carrying Bramhall Moor Lane. The works of Mirrlees Blackstone dominate the background.

15th FEBRUARY 1952 ● G. COLTAS

The Nottingham - Liverpool train crosses Chester Road at speed in the hands of a Nottingham Stanier Class 5, No **44841**. Shortly after this date, the working often produced one of the home depot's Jubilees, which were considered strangers and therefore an added attraction to the trainspotting fraternity. On this particular Saturday, a Nottingham loco, LMS Compoound No 40929 had already passed by on its way to Aintree with an excursion, for this was Grand National day!

7th APRIL 1951 ● T. LEWIS

The Rising Sun Inn Tram Terminus. Both Stockport and Manchester cars are in evidence. The nearer enclosed example, No **26,** was built locally by Stockport Corporation in 1929 whilst behind is Manchester's No **1035,** one of a series of enclosed bogie types numbered 1004 - 1053, which were built by English Electric at Preston during the 1927 - 28 period. It is working service No 35 and will be soon be ready to return to Manchester once the conductor has changed the monkey (or reversed the trolley pole). Meanwhile a Midland 2P 4-4-0 heads south towards Disley Tunnel over the 230 yard long, 13 span viaduct on the ex-Midland main line.

c.1930 ● W.A. CAMWELL

Taken from the same pavement as the above photograph but over thirty years later and looking in the opposite direction towards Stockport. North Western bus No **649** (KDB 649) takes the Macclesfield road off the roundabout with service No 425. Although the destination blind shows Chapel Street School, Hazel Grove, the vehicle is transporting children on their late afternoon homewardbound journeys. Note the cyclist complete with trilby and bike clips standing alongside the *Rising Sun* public house, which although temporarily without its hanging sign, has lost none of its olde-worlde charm.

c.1965 ● ABCROSS

Stanier 8F 2-8-0 No 48224 approaches Cheadle Village Junction with a lengthy train of empties from Northwich to Dewsnap Sidings.

11th FEBRUARY 1968 ● P. JORDAN

CHEADLE VILLAGE JUNCTION

The view looking east. The lines to the right offered a connection with the Buxton branch at Davenport Junction, nearly one mile distant. The sidings serving the local wagon repair works can be seen beyond which is a footbridge connecting Petersburg Road with the Bridge Hall Estate in nearby Adswood. The lines ahead are for Edgeley Junction which formed a triangle with Davenport Junction. The chimney behind the signalbox stands 312ft high and belongs to Sykes' Bleach Works. Founded in 1793, it had its own rail connection by 1846, delivering cloth twice daily. The branch, somewhat curiously, ran from behind Edgeley shed, skirted two reservoirs and crossed two roads on the level in the process before entering the works. It closed in the early 1950's with the factory going a few years later. Little trace now remains, save the two reservoirs which form part of a local conservation area.

27th JULY 1963 ● G. HARROP

The Lancashire & North West Branch of the RCTS organised a railtour covering 85 miles of branch and goods lines around the Greater Manchester area. These lines were either threatened with closure or about to lose their passenger service. After departing from Manchester London Road with its five coach train, ex L&YR 2-4-2T No **50644** (8B, Warrington Dallam) made for the Bury and Bolton areas before passing again through London Road's through platforms (ex-MSJ&A line) bound for the Stockport area. The train is pictured six hours after departure time, passing Cheadle Village Junction. On the final stage of the journey, the veteran performed heroics between Stockport Edgeley and London Road covering the 5.9 miles in just 9 minutes 25 seconds, reaching a top speed of 57.5mph at Longsight.   **26th JULY 1953** ● **B.K.B. GREEN**

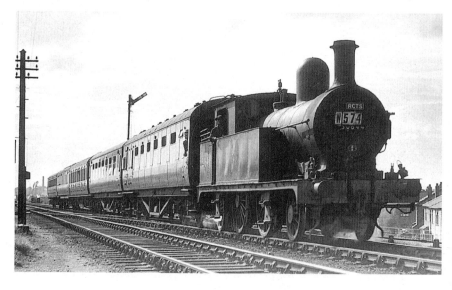

THE KHYBER

A 6 car Birmingham R C W multiple unit crosses the North West Frontier, or the *Khyber Pass* as it was affectionately known. The ex LNWR main line between Edgeley Junction and Adswood Sidings was in fact the border. Overhead catenary now spans the four running lines in the shallow cutting beyond which stands Bridge Hall school with Sykes's chimney also prominent. This view looking west is from Bakery Bridge, a notorious blind spot at the junction of Stockholm and Adswood Roads.

26th JULY 1963 ● G. HARROP

Driver Ricky Reeves and Fireman Mark Meeks from Trafford Park Depot bring BR Standard Class 3 2-6-2T No **82003** off the Khyber with a *'Cotton Spinners Railtour'* organised by the Locomotive Club of Great Britain (LCGB). Resplendent in unlined green livery, the loco arrived at Patricroft Depot during March 1965 having enjoyed a short 13 year life working mainly over ex-GWR lines. It was unofficially named 'Fanny' by the Patricroft men and carried the earlier 'lion & wheel' totem until withdrawal from there in December 1966.

16th APRIL 1966 ● G. HARROP

A pleasing study of a pair of Home signals at Cheadle Village Junction. That on the left controls the line from Edgeley Junction. At its base to the left of the white notice board is an ex-LNWR ground signal which, unlike its more modern LMS counterpart, pivoted round on its base so that the top half of the unit rotated through 90°. This signal controlled the outlet to the long siding between this point and Davenport Junction. Hughes Crab 2-6-0 No **42941** is waiting on the bi-directional single line which was worked by a set of Webb and Thompson miniature train staff instruments from Cheadle Village Junction and Davenport Junction signalboxes. **16th APRIL 1966 ● G. HARROP**

BUS VARIETY IN THE EDGELEY DISTRICT

Stockport Corporation had a sizeable fleet of Massey Bros bodied wartime Guy Arabs, but by October 1963 only six remained in service. This example, fleet No **211** (JA 7611) is in its latter day condition working service No 31 from Mersey Square to Stockport Edgeley Fold whose terminus lay immediately beyond Alexandra Park off Castle Street.

c.1958 ● P. SHACKCLOTH COLLECTION

One of the most interesting routes in the Borough was that which was jointly operated by Stockport Corporation, Ashton Corporation and SHMD (Stalybridge, Hyde, Mossley and Dukinfield). Three services, numbers 29, 30 and 31, ran between Edgeley and Ashton. Number 29 went from Edgeley (Cheadle Old Road) to Hyde via Gee Cross. Number 30 from Edgeley (Cheadle Old Road) to Ashton via Dowson Road, Hyde, and Dukinfield. Number 31 ran from Edgeley (Petersburg Road) to Ashton by the same route. A representative of the SHMD fleet, No **79** (279 ATU) is a Daimler CVG6 built in 1957. It is setting out on its journey down Dale Street and is passing the reservoir once associated with the Sykes Bleach Works. The dormobile further down the road is at a point where the branch line serving the bleach works would have crossed the road on the level.

c.1962 ● M. KEELEY COLLECTION

Leaving Edgeley Junction, Standard 9F 2-10-0 No 92069 brings a train of coal bound for Garston towards Cheadle Village Junction on the last day of steam operation at Edgeley. Two days later, Speke Junction shed (8C) closed and No 92069 was withdrawn. The bridge in the background carries Stockholm Road which led to an area known locally as 'Little Siberia'. The property above the embankment fronts on to Petersburg Road which paralleled the line for some distance. Other road names selected by the Council included Vienna, Moscow, Berlin, Brussels and Finland. Stockport is synonymous with hat making, the origins of which go back well before the advent of steam and a great percentage of the local workforce found employment in both this and the railway industry. One of the town's many hat manufacturers was J. Woodrow and Sons, whose factory and chimney dominate the skyline beyond the train.

4th MAY 1968 ● J. CLOUGH

DIVERTED TRAFFIC

The elegant profile of Jubilee 4-6-0 No 45645 *Collingwood* is somewhat obscured by the eaves of Cheadle Village Junction Signalbox as it passes with the 10.15am Holyhead - Manchester Victoria, diverted via Stockport rather than travelling by way of the normal route through Chester via Earlestown. No 45645 was a long time resident of nearby Patricroft depot but seldom seen in the Stockport area. Prior to October 1952 it would have been an even rarer sight as *Collingwood* was a Corkerhill (Glasgow) loco!

27th JULY 1963 ● G. HARROP

Standard Class Fives were also generally considered to be unusual visitors to Stockport. Another Patricroft loco, No **73011**, brings returning holidaymakers from Abergele, with the 10.30am to Manchester Victoria, similarly diverted. Cheadle Village Junction signalbox is in the distance. The line between Edgeley and Northenden Junctions saw a considerable volume of freight traffic but local passenger services were withdrawn as long ago as 1917. During the summer months it offered a convenient link between the towns of Yorkshire and Chester, the gateway to the North Wales coast. It also became an important diversionary route for trains which would normally use the direct route to Crewe and beyond during the latter lines' period of installation of electrification and re-signalling works.

27th JULY 1963 ● G. HARROP

Another Jubilee passing through Stockport on the same day was No **45708 *Resolution*.** This train, from Llandudno to Leeds was scheduled to traverse this route, having arrived by way of Chester, Helsby, Frodsham, Warrington High Level Junction, Arpley, Broadheath, Skelton Junction and Northenden Junction. The loco hails from Farnley Junction, Leeds and plenty of coal is still in evidence. The journey over the Cheshire plain would have hardly taxed the crew so far but the harder work was to come on the final stage of the journey over the Pennine hills and through Standedge Tunnel.

27th JULY 1963 ● G. HARROP

The Fairfield Loop was a sparsely used route which offered a connection from the Great Central's London Road - Sheffield line at Fairfield with the Midland's South District Line at Chorlton Junction - a distance of nearly 10 miles. In the latter years of steam, the only important passenger trains using it were the boat trains connecting Liverpool Central with Hull & Harwich after reversing at Manchester Central. Fairburn Class 4 2-6-4T No **42050** is about to pass the recently constructed Reddish Electric Depot with such a train. The Trafford Park loco will be relieved at Guide Bridge by electric traction. Interestingly, the Ordnance Survey map shows the Borough boundary bisecting the easterly end of the shed yard! **c.1959** ● **T. LEWIS**

STOCKPORT EDGELEY
LOCOS AT WORK

Fowler 2-6-4T No 42379 emerges from Standedge Tunnel with a train which may well be the 12.35pm Stalybridge to Leeds City stopper. According to the Working Timetable, empty coaching stock left Stockport to arrive at Stalybridge at 11.30am. The train then travelled via Greenfield before crossing to the slow line at Diggle Junction to Huddersfield. The fast line from Stalybridge to Huddersfield via Mossley is to the right. The circular sign carrying the letter 'C' indicates 'Commencement of Temporary Speed Restrictions' and was oil lit.

12th APRIL 1952 ● **E. R. MORTEN**

OVER THE PENNINES

A regular working over the Pennine hills took one of the Edgeley tank engines to Leeds City on a stopping passenger train. No **42391** is recorded on its return journey approaching at a rather sedate speed near Diggle. The Fowler Tanks rarely ventured off the beaten track but on the morning of Monday, 10th April 1961, sister loco No 42343 was observed passing through Birmingham Snow Hill with freight in the Wolverhampton direction. Three days later she worked the 5.10pm Snow Hill to Knowle & Dorridge before returning with the 6.25pm to Birmingham Moor Street.

c. 1958 ● **J. DAVENPORT**

The New Mills shunt left Edgeley sidings at 6.05am. About four wagons of coal would be deposited at Davenport and the train would be left on the 'block road' adjacent to the Co-op sidings at Adswood, hence the train's nickname - the 'Divi Shunt'. It would then proceed to New Mills where the crew would have their breakfast after shunting had been completed. The return journey took in Disley goods to drop off empties and take out paper from Bowaters. Davenport was shunted and coal empties taken out, a procedure which was repeated at the Co-op sidings at Adswood. Edgeley Sidings were reached at 2.00pm from where the loco retired to the depot for servicing. 9B's flagship engine, Jubilee 4-6-0 No **45596 Bahamas** stands beneath the signalbox at New Mills Newtown whilst working the turn for which it was regularly diagrammed during 1965.

MARCH 1965 ● P. SHACKCLOTH COLLECTION

Ashton Junction, Guide Bridge. Recently erected catenary straddles the complex of lines in this easterly view. Ex-LNWR 0-8-0 No **49281** wheezes its way towards Guide Bridge Station with a mixed freight, probably bound for Jubilee Sidings, Heaton Norris. A number of 'Super D's' were fitted for steam heating which was a necessary requirement when handling the banana trains from Liverpool docks. Two unidentified Gorton locos are also in attendance. The tender of an ex-GCR J11 0-6-0 can be glimpsed on the left within Brookside Sidings whilst a member of the C13 4-4-2 Tank Class and stock await entry to the station, probably prior to working a local train to Oldham Clegg Street via the OA&GB line.

13th JUNE 1954 ● B.K.B. GREEN

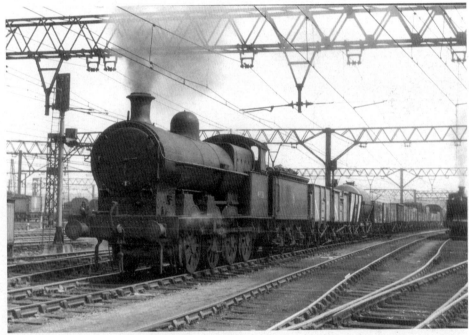

GUIDE BRIDGE

Whilst awaiting the signal to return light engine to its home depot, the crew of Stockport Edgeley's Stanier Jubilee 4-6-0 No **45632 Tonga** kindly allow a couple of young enthusiasts to 'cab' the loco. 'Tonga' stands just beyond the deep shadow cast on Platform 2 from the overbridge carrying Guide Lane. By the early 1960's, the whole station was a shadow of its former self. Local services over the Fallowfield line and those over the OA&GB to Oldham had ceased in 1958 and 1959 respectively. The electrified passenger service over Woodhead from Manchester Piccadilly to Sheffield Victoria outlasted steam by a mere 16 months, ending in January 1970.

23rd MAY 1964 ● G. COLTAS

A quartet of the diminutive Ivatt Class 2 2-6-2T's (Nos 41202/4/20/33) arrived in August 1965 from Wales to replace the newer BR counterparts (Nos 84013/4/7/26). They found work on station pilot duty and local parcels trains. No **41202** is up against the buffers in Platform 2 at Manchester Victoria Station, having worked round via Denton and Droylsden Junctions. This particular loco had a chequered career. It went new in 1946 to Abergavenny where it worked passenger trains to Merthyr along the ex-LNWR 'Heads of the Valleys' line. Between March 1955 and August 1962 it was perhaps unique in working out of all three Bristol Depots: Bath Road, Barrow Road and St Philips Marsh. Short spells followed at Shrewsbury, Croes Newydd and Llandudno Junction before taking up final residence on English soil. Sister loco No 41204 was employed by the RCTS for a brake van tour of Staffordshire branches on 29th October 1966 but all four were withdrawn from service the following month.

JUNE 1966 ● B. CRAMER

Stanier 2-6-2T No 40071 approaches Park Bridge with a Stockport to Oldham Clegg Street local. The journey took 30 minutes with passengers also travelling to or from Heaton Norris, Reddish South, Denton, Ashton Oldham Road and Park Bridge benefitting from the service. The closure of the OA&GB line in the summer of 1959 brought about its demise. By the end of the decade, Edgeley men were left with little regular passenger work.

c. 1958 ● J. DAVENPORT

HEATON MERSEY LOCOS AT WORK

The mainstay of Heaton Mersey's allocation during BR days were the Stanier 8F 2-8-0's. They were regularly employed taking coal to Garston Docks and returning the empties to either Godley Junction or Gowhole. They were also frequent visitors to Rowsley and Hasland depots after working freight over the ex-Midland lines. A long standing member, No **48503** runs tender first towards Chinley with a mixed goods train.

May 1961 ● P. SHACKCLOTH COLLECTION

A four year course studying Art and Design at Stockport College offered the author perfect scope to escape to places like Baguley during official 'sketching' periods. It also offered the opportunity to photograph the multitude of freight trains still traversing this very busy section of railway. In its heyday, traffic between Northenden and Skelton Junctions over the CLC was amongst the most intensive in the country, with the passage of a train on average every 7 minutes during peak periods. Local passenger services between Stockport Tiviot Dale and Warrington Central, however, had ceased on 30th November 1964. Taking up 'sketching' positions on the abandoned island platform, fellow art students Dave Jessop and Steve Clayton witness the passage of another Heaton Mersey 8F, No **48252**, rumbling through in the Stockport direction with a mixed goods train.

26th APRIL 1968 ● P. SHACKCLOTH

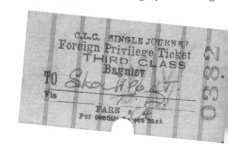

With the withdrawal of local services from Liverpool Central and Warrington to Stockport Tiviot Dale in November 1964, Heaton Mersey's Passenger Link were left to perform duties over the Manchester South District Line, supplemented by occasional excursion and special workings. One of the depot's Ivatt Class 4 2-6-0's No **43033** stands at Manchester Central awaiting departure with the 12.10pm SO to Cheadle Heath. The train occupies Platform 8 which was outside the train shed which towers over the canopy. An engine release road existed between Platforms 8 and 9 in common with three other pairs within the station proper. (Platform 7 was a bay). The stock is hard up against the buffers, suggesting that the loco has either reversed or set back its four coach train.

17th JULY 1965 ● D. R. MORGAN

STOCKPORT EDGELEY LOCOS ON RAILTOUR DUTY

Two of Edgeley's 'Britannia' Pacifics, Nos 70004 *William Shakespeare* and 70015 *Apollo* were often employed on rail tour duties. The pair were kept in fine condition by the shed staff who had fitted a makeshift front numberplate to No 70015. *Apollo* is pictured approaching Cornholme Signalbox on the 1 in 65 climb to Copy Pit Summit hauling a 'Lancastrian Rail Tour' organised by the *Railway Correspondence and Travel Society*, reporting number IT55. Departing from Manchester Victoria at 10.00am, the train travelled by way of Bolton, Bury, Todmorden, Padiham, Feniscowles, Bolton, Lostock Junction, Hindley, Standish Junction, Lostock Hall, Burscough, Southport, Liverpool and Manchester Piccadilly, before returning at 5.44pm.

19th MARCH 1967 ● E. F. BENTLEY

The Edgeley men were particularly fond of their Fowler Class 4 2-6-4 tanks, none more so than No **42343**. It was kept in excellent condition and was popularly employed on a number of railtours. Seen here pausing at Hartington whilst working a SLS trip bound for the Leicestershire area, the outward journey from Manchester Piccadilly had been via Stockport, Buxton, Ashbourne and the Uttoxeter avoiding line, returning via Burton on Trent and the Churnet Valley. This loco also worked the 'Staffordshire Potter' *(featured elsewhere)* and on 7th August 1965 worked a LCGB 'Brake Van Special' of branch lines in the North Manchester area. This, however, came after its unfortunate transfer to Springs Branch, Wigan two months earlier. 42343 was withdrawn from Trafford Park in October 1965 but if ever there had been a candidate for preservation, it was surely this loco.

8th SEPTEMBER 1962 ● G. HARROP

A Stephenson Locomotive Society 'Lakes and Fells' Railtour gave 9B's remaining Jubilee 4-6-0 No **45596** *Bahamas* another opportunity of passenger work on the main line. Departing from Manchester Exchange, the train ran via Bolton and Blackburn to Hellifield where *Bahamas* was relieved by the celebrated Gresley A3 Pacific already in preservation, No 4472 *Flying Scotsman*. A snow blizzard in April was unprecedented but this made for dramatic photography. *Bahamas* was turned out in immaculate condition by the shed staff who had become increasingly proud of their last 'Jub'. Later in the day she worked the final leg of the railtour retracing the outward journey back to Manchester.

2nd APRIL 1966 ● P. SHACKCLOTH COLLECTION

RAILTOURS PASSING THROUGH STOCKPORT

A pair of Newton Heath 'Jinties' were employed on a '3 Counties Railtour', organised by the 'Manchester Rail Travel Society'. The 'Pilot' engine was No **47202,** one of the early Johnson 3F 0-6-0's fitted with condensing apparatus for work on the London Metropolitan widened lines. The other was No **47383** which is perhaps fortunate to survive in preservation. The owners of this loco had originally earmarked No 47202, but a flaw in the frame and the resultant bent buffer beam precluded this. She was withdrawn soon afterwards. The train is seen on arrival at Edgeley's No 1 platform where the engines detached before running in tandem to the shed for servicing. The 60ft turntable accommodated both veterans in what was probably a unique operation.

26th NOVEMBER 1966 ● P. HUTCHINSON

No 45110 at Edgeley Stn.

SINCE PRESERVED ● B. CRICK

This particular RCTS railtour, jointly operated by the 'Lancashire North West & Merseyside Branch' and the 'Severn Valley Railway', resulted in the use of six different locos on 20th April 1968. They were Nos D3180, 45110, 44949, 73134, 73069 and 48773. The train ran from Birmingham New Street to Liverpool Lime Street via Stockport, Buxton, Chinley, Romiley, Stalybridge, Copy Pit, Bury, Rochdale, the Oldham Loop and Denton Junction.

No 48773 passing Edgeley Junction No 2 Signalbox.

SINCE PRESERVED ● P. SHACKCLOTH COLLECTION

STOCKPORT IN THE DAYS OF STEAM

FRONT COVER. **The majesty of British steam.** One of Stanier's masterpieces, an immaculate 'Princess Coronation' or 'Duchess' Class 4-6-2 No **46247** *City of Liverpool* from Camden depot, glides elegantly into Stockport Edgeley Station with an afternoon Crewe to Manchester London Road local. Ex-works locos were frequently observed on running in turns such as this. In No 46247's case, she had entered Crewe Works week ending 26th May 1951 for General Repair before re-emerging on 15th June. The sun nicely shows off the 'Duchess's' black livery with straw lining, a condition she retained until February 1954 when the loco was repainted in Brunswick Green, fully lined out. A final livery change saw her adopting BR Maroon in May 1958. The sloping top of the smokebox front indicated the Pacific as being one of those originally built with streamline casing.

JUNE 1951 ● T. MORGAN

BACK COVER. **Fowler/Hughes 'Crab' 2-6-0 No 13188.** Stockport Edgeley Depot.
26th JULY 1931 ● L. HANSON

Stockport Corporation Crossley No **226** (JA 7626). Heaton Lane Depot.
1964 ● D. YOUNG COLLECTION

Jubilee 4-6-0 No **45629** *Straits Settlements.* Parrs Wood.
1955 ● B.K.B. GREEN

Stockport Corporation Tramways Car No **27.** Armoury Square.
23rd MARCH 1949 ● R.B. PARR

Stanier 8F 2-8-0 No **48168.** Heaton Mersey Depot.
6th DECEMBER 1967 ● P. SHACKCLOTH

Royal Scot 4-6-0 No **46129** *The Scottish Horse.* Stockport Edgeley Station.
1950 ● A. BENDELL

Steam
IMAGE